Nell Hill's Decorating Secrets

Nell Hill's Decorating Secrets

Easy and Inspiring Ways
to Bring Style into Your Home

MARY CAROL GARRITY

Photography by Bryan E. McCay

BULFINCH PRESS

New York • Boston

Bulfinch Press

Hachette Book Group USA

1271 Avenue of the Americas, New York, NY 10020

Visit our Web site at www.bulfinchpress.com

First Edition

Second printing, 2006

Nell Hill's® is a registered trademark of Nell Hill's Corporation.

ISBN 10 : 0-8212-2903-6

ISBN 13 : 978-0-8212-2903-6

Library of Congress Control Number 2004102957

PRODUCED BY SMALLWOOD & STEWART, INC.,

New York City

Designed by Alexis Siroc

Printed in Singapore

To my coworkers at Nell Hill's, G. Diebolt's, Garrity's, and our warehouse. Their talent and dedication made this book and so many other things possible.

The Nell Hill's
Approach

~~~~~~

*E*very year thousands of visitors come to my three home furnishings

stores in the small riverside town of Atchison, Kansas. One of my

greatest pleasures is to talk about each person's decorating plans and ideas and

translate them into fabrics, furnishings, art, and accessories that turn

their vision into bedrooms and kitchens, living rooms, and studies

that they enjoy. For me, this experience is always fresh and exciting —

I'm introduced to new people as well as old friends and, in the process, get a

wonderful education both about the way people like to live and how

best to achieve it — lessons I want to share in this book.

Most often, the warm, interesting homes I admire haven't had a particular look or style imposed upon them by a professional. They have evolved — and continue to evolve — from the people who live there. When I visit such homes, I get a real feeling for the interests and lifestyles of the occupants as well as a sense that things are the way they are thanks to imagination rather than expense. (And, perhaps, that is the most important secret of all — that a stylish, comfortable home does not have to cost a lot.) I see in all of these homes a willingness to mix formal with informal elements and new with old, layered in fresh, clever ways to give each room interest and character. It's this kind of personal, creative touch that makes your home different from anyone else's, that makes it your own, and that I consider a hallmark of my approach to decorating.

Generally, I'm not one to subscribe to decorating rules. Too often, I think they lead to rooms that are impractical or contrived, places that may look good in photographs but not anywhere I'd want to curl up and read a book. Besides, the truth is that there is no one way to decorate that suits everyone. The homes of three friends — in Kansas City, Sylvia Zinn and Nan Sigman, and in Atchison, Neil and Gretchen Sullivan — included in these

pages are vivid proof of just that: Each achieves just the right mix of comfort, style, and creativity in quite different ways.

The secrets I have gathered in this book are not rules to be followed inflexibly but starting points for you to shape and adapt and, above all, experiment with to suit your own taste and needs. I'm constantly changing things around in my house and trying out new arrangements, and I encourage you to do the same — it's by far the most effective way to discover what's best for you. I hope this book inspires you to do some experimenting of your own.

First Impressions

The front door should be the centerpiece of the exterior of your house,

setting a tone for everything inside, and extending a greeting to all who

drop by. To give it presence, I always like to frame the entrance with

some sort of commanding planting, either tall topiaries or large urns overflowing

with flowers and a drapery of vines. It will make even a simple doorway

seem wider, grander, and more important. If you have steps up to the door,

consider flanking the bottom stair with containers of seasonal plantings

or some garden statuary. Or place small pots of plants in baskets on each stair.

So long as they are well-balanced, the ingredients needn't be fancy —

gourds and pumpkins, heaps of pinecones, tall plumes of decorative grasses, or

masses of geraniums or petunias will help roll out a carpet of welcome.

Decorating my front door for a special event
or seasonal celebration is one of my favorite
projects. It doesn't have to take a lot of time, and
I like the chance to create something whimsical.
Instead of a solitary wreath at Christmas, I might
mix three smaller ones of boxwood, bittersweet,
and spruce hung from different-colored ribbons;
or I might create a garland made from vintage
Christmas ornaments. Think of the door as if it
were a wall of a room—a place to hang a trio
of mirrors or evocative images in small frames,
perhaps prints of autumn leaves encircled by real
ones, or even a photograph of the guest of
honor at a party.

*On an all-white house, I love
the contrast of a door painted
a strong color — or even black.
It just magnetizes the eye.*

front door
3 ways

Even in the shelter of our porch, arrangements must weather the Midwestern elements, so if they're going to stay up for any length of time, I select sturdy materials, such as dried grasses or branches with brightly colored berries. These days it's possible to find beautiful and convincing artificial foliage as well.

✳ **1 TO SET THE MOOD** for a summer party, *left,* I brought out some small botanical paintings to greet guests. A lush sheaf of beribboned greenery adds a verdant frame.

✳ **2 A MIX OF FROSTED FERNS,** plumes, and pinecones, *above,* gives this late-fall arrangement a rich weave of different textures and shapes.

✳ **3 THERE'S SOMETHING** about floral plates that seems to say spring, *opposite,* and those with perforated rims make hanging easy. Grouping three or more tends to be much more interesting than one or two.

A simple, inexpensive mirror, *opposite*, adds some sparkle to a spill of ribboned grapevines. Just inside my front door I created an arrangement that echoes the same colors: This great burst of red berries and mixed leaves in a red ceramic vase, *below*, uses completely different materials to bring the same autumn mood indoors.

I want guests to feel welcome even before they've taken their coats off, so the entry hall is especially important to me, although it is just a transitional area. In my friend Gretchen's home, a large mirror flanked by a pair of tall lamps gives this space presence, *above*. A rich, embracing paint color, such as deep red, *opposite*, lends a warmth and depth to furniture and paintings.

Even if your front door opens directly into a room, create a sense of an entry, using a screen, lighting, or a piece of furniture.

A Place to Relax

Gone are the days when the living room or front parlor was just a formal showpiece, kept only for special occasions. These days it's both more practical and more personal: a place where we can equally settle in with a book or enjoy an evening of lively conversation with friends surrounded by personal touches that express our lives and interests.

Since this is a room for entertaining company, it should be sociably arranged, with lots of flexibility in the seating: Chairs should be close but not on top of one another, so that people can converse and move around freely. Besides the traditional conversation core of sofa and two upholstered chairs, I like to have a good-sized upholstered ottoman that seats two or more to pull into the group; with a tray on top, it can also serve as a coffee table.

I feel most at home in a room that seems to have grown naturally, rather than one that's been "done" all at once, with everything just so. Once the major pieces — sofa, chairs, bookshelves — are in place, let other furnishings, pillows, and art find their homes around them. Although I like a sense of visual balance, such as by enhancing the wall behind the sofa with a grouping of pictures, too much planning can result in a static, "matchy" look. I avoid this by including a variety of fabrics, mixing in some offbeat end tables, and scattering a few pretty table lamps that aren't in pairs. Then I let things evolve. A room, after all, should be allowed to grow and change as seasons and families do.

Add some vertical emphasis to balance strong horizontal shapes and raise the eye level. A mixed grouping of pictures will do the trick.

TEXTILES ARE great civilizers of the spaces we live in. We count on upholstery, cushions, and curtains to add softness and pattern, to make a room more interesting and inviting. I always enjoy playing with swatches and assembling a family of fabrics that will get along happily together but are just varied enough to entertain the eye. If there is a strong-patterned rug or a lot of art in the room, I will often lean toward neutrals for furniture fabrics so they won't compete and save the prints for decorative pillows or a side chair. My own living-room upholstery is white (actually, three slightly different shades of white), which gives me endless opportunity to change the room by simply changing the accents, from throw pillows to the slipcover on an ottoman.

A pleasing mix of patterns is as important to me as a good color palette.

armchairs
3 ways

A special little armchair can have so much character and is an asset anywhere — in a bedroom or an entrance hall, even by the kitchen phone. Of course, soft seat cushions and back pillows should make it inviting, but you can combine fabric and trim to give it a one-of-a-kind personality.

1 COMBINING TWO cheerful cotton prints, such as a toile bolster with red checks, *left,* was my friend Sylvia's choice for relaxing the look of her antique chair.

2 DRESSMAKER DETAILS transform a standard armchair upholstered in plain white cotton, *above.* From bows on the back cushion to the matching trim, it sparkles with whimsy. Note the many ways in which Sylvia used one check — as the pillow border, as trim, as fanciful antimacassars, even on the diminutive ottoman.

3 WICKER IS AT HOME in almost any room these days. An equestrian print, *opposite,* gives this chair a look equally suitable for a study or a porch setting. The crisscrossed fabric picks up the woven pattern on the chair arm.

Big checks not only suit the scale of this sofa, above, but also give
a nod to its Provençal lines. To gentle this strong statement, pillows of sunny
toiles lend delicacy and a welcome splash of citron. As an extra flourish at
the base, the twist cording is scalloped.

*A bold color or upholstery pattern on the sofa
sets the tone for the rest of the room.*

dressing the sofa
3 ways

I like to be able to change the look of my sofa easily. With any neutral color, such as beige, dark green, or navy, I simply change out the throw pillows — or, in some cases, just their covers.

✳ **1 MY LITTLE WHITE SOFA** is a chameleon in washed damask, a fabric I like for its muted, natural look. Dressy silk bolsters with tassels and demurely printed pillows, *above*, play up its pale complexion; the tiny tapestry pillow in the center ties in the dark tones of the screen behind.

✳ **2 THE SECRET TO MIXING** patterns is keeping to a single color scheme, *right*. A rich, almost lavish look is created by layering pillows

of golden silk, burgundy velvet, and petit-point, and a pair finished with ball fringe.

✳ **3 A SIMPLE TRIO** dresses my sofa in springtime, *left*, to keep the mood light and cheerful. Like pictures, decorative pillows look best with some framing, such as these ruffled edges and fringed borders.

lighting

THE WARM GLOW of lamplight is like a "welcome home" at the end of a busy day. In fact, chasing away the shadows was one of my first priorities when we renovated our old house, because there's something about a badly lit room that never feels right, no matter how beautifully it may be decorated. There are lots of modern designs for lighting, but I admit I'm something of a traditionalist — not only because I have a soft spot for pretty table lamps and chandeliers but also because they suit the style of our house. Table lamps especially contribute so much to a room. They can be handsome sculptural accents, stand ready to focus on a book or task, or simply add an inviting glimmer where one least expects it. I'm a strong advocate of dimmers, particularly in the dining room, where we turn the lights romantically low and let the flickering candles provide illumination and atmosphere.

Several table lamps provide more atmospheric and decorative lighting than a single bright source.

Nell Hill's Decorating Secrets

Hung above a secretary that was too small for a table lamp, *opposite*, this tiny chandelier isn't centered over anything—but suddenly the once-dark corner glows. *Below,* a stroke of inventiveness turned an old floor lamp into a "chandelier lamp."

Chandeliers can add a touch of the romance to the most unexpected places — the kitchen, the bathroom, or even a study.

lampshades
3 ways

The right shade suits not only the shape, style, and size of the lamp but also the room in which it's used. When you go shopping for a shade, take the lamp with you. Look at how each selection pairs with the base and how different colors and fabrics, from parchment to silk to linen, dramatically affect the quality of the light.

※ **1 CRISP WHITE LINEN** on a translucent drum shade, *left,* becomes a bright, modern accent in a room and creates a general, diffuse light.

※ **2 THE FLARED BELL** of this silk shade, *above,* adds width to a slim base and is a dressy choice. Silk always has a warm luminescence, and the amber tint of this shade casts an especially mellow glow.

※ **3 AN OPAQUE SHADE** casts a very directional light, almost like a spotlight, so even this diminutive lamp is a strong accent in my living room, *opposite.* A dear friend added a golden looped fringe, which softens the effect.

side tables
3 ways

If you need an end table, create one! That's what I tell customers who want something "different from the usual." Consider covering a weathered garden urn or low birdbath with glass to introduce a new texture to the room, or use a footstool topped with a tray. I'm a great fan of old leather suitcases and vintage hatboxes, too — and they'll do wonders for your storage needs.

※**1 LOOK TO THE GARDEN** for original decorative accents — urns, birdbaths, and terracotta pots all contribute an appealing patina indoors. This garden pedestal, *opposite*, which held flowers in summer, finds a whole new life in winter as a handsome little side table.

※**2 STACKED BASKETS,** *above*, lend a casual note to the living room. Books are at hand, and magazines are out of sight in the deep upper basket. Best of all, by stacking you can achieve just the height you want.

※**3 MY FAVORITE TRAYS** are always out where they can be seen. One provides a level surface for a side table, *right*, and a perfect platform for a collection of old boxes.

mantels

I'M ALL IN FAVOR of liberating the mantel. For too long, people have put them in a decorative straitjacket, unsure how to dress them other than with one big picture or mirror flanked by a pair of candlesticks. But for such a significant place in a room, I much prefer groupings that are personal, seasonal, and fluid. Instead of one over-the-mantel painting or photograph, how about several grouped in a balanced arrangement? In my home, favorite accessories, from different-sized silver cups to figurines and ceramic boxes, keep bidding for their turn in the spotlight. Sometimes I'll just start with a color combination in mind, say blue and yellow, then hunt up a mix of objects that will fit the bill.

Avoid exact symmetry — an arrangement that is perfectly balanced appears static and dull.

mantels
3 ways

Small tweakings — just switching or taking away a few items — can be as refreshing as major alterations. Keep in mind that the mantel isn't a separate place but part of the room and should complement its general style.

※ **1 HIGH DRAMA,** *opposite,* is created by the unexpected use of a wood-and-cane screen. Alone, so strong an accent might be too imposing, but here it's softened by colorful framed butterflies and botanical prints.

※ **2 ONE LOVELY MAIN PIECE** can inspire companion items. A delicately sprigged mirror in faded white, *above,* suggested a white-and-gold autumn palette and some favorite ironstone pieces.

※ **3 IN SPRINGTIME,** *right,* the same mirror is flanked by floral paintings and, to pick up the blue wall color, a little porcelain plate. If you're using picture frames, mix vertical and horizontal shapes to add interest.

art

IT'S NO SECRET that art has the power to inspire us and enhance our world. What we sometimes forget is that even the humblest arrangement — whether a single engraving or a pair of black-and-white photographs or a collection of a child's watercolors — can bring great charm and character to any room. Best of all, so many things take on a new life when framed or hung on a wall. Most of us probably have more possibilities tucked away in our closets than we realize, from old handwritten family recipes to ornate small hand-mirrors to scraps of vintage lace. Placed artfully, these can be wonderful choices for waking up a blank corner or plain wall.

But main rooms aren't the only places for art. I like to use prints or photographs to lead the way up my staircase or down a long hall, or stack them up to the ceiling to offset the diminutive dimensions of a small powder room. To avoid the predictable, try mixing up styles of frames, for example, or combining pictures with graphic platters or a single large mirror.

Hanging pictures just above eye level visually raises the ceiling height.

plates and pictures
3 ways

A successful arrangement needn't be perfectly symmetrical, but it should have a pleasing sense of balance and harmony. This is easiest to pull off, of course, when everything is alike in shape or size or color palette, but it's far more engaging to the eye when they aren't.

❋1 **A COLLECTION OF ENGRAVINGS** gathered over time is not, strictly speaking, a set, *left*, or they weren't, until they were framed and matted almost identically.

❋2 **SOMETIMES ARRANGEMENTS** can be used to add presence to an architectural feature, *above*. This mixed group of paintings and prints create an attractive frame around my daughter's bedroom door.

❋3 **THESE TOLE TRAYS** collected by my friend Sylvia form a marvelous grouping that also serves to frame a seating area in the corner of her large living room, *opposite*.

collections

WHOEVER SAID that the whole is greater than the sum of its parts must have been a collector. Like many people, I'm drawn magnetically (sometimes compulsively!) to acquire specific things that speak to me; I can barely resist china decorated with birds, pretty silver candlesticks, and exquisite little wood boxes. Some of my finds are precious, others merely appealing, but they all have greater impact as part of a collection than they would have alone.

True collections begin from the heart. They lend personal warmth to a home and make it different from anyone else's. They're not about price or value, though they can sometimes be about rarity. To me they're also about the excitement of the hunt, the thrill of discovery, and most of all, the pleasure of living with the things we love.

*If you love something, get it.
You'll always find a place for it.*

A substantial collection deserves its own showcase — an étagère, Welsh dresser, or, as on these pages, a tall, brass-edged baker's rack. Rather than crowd her antique silver pieces together, my friend Nan set them out well-spaced amid a veritable garden of ivy topiaries, *opposite*. A similar airy rack permits a stunning collection of large china treasures to be on view together, *above*.

collections
3 ways

To help treasures that caught your eye catch the eye of others, make sure they benefit from good placement and lighting. Details of small items, which might be lost on a high shelf, show best at eye level — on a mantel, for example, or grouped on a side table and illuminated by a lamp.

❋ 1 **THEMED COLLECTIONS,** such as pink-and-white teacups, Western ephemera, or this bee-inspired grouping, always make for an intriguing mix, *opposite*.

❋ 2 **SHEEP SAFELY REST,** under the glow of a shepherdess lamp, *above*, giving a touch of color to this monochrome flock. The lamp and floral majolica plate, all in the cheerful spirit of pastoral pleasures, further define the low-lying collection.

❋ 3 **SHELL ART** has been popular for centuries. One collector sought out varied items in similar hues and pavéd style for this seashore-themed display, *right*.

displays

I CAN'T HELP treating objects I love as characters in a visual play. Actually, in many plays, because the collection of characters can act many parts in many different plays every time I rearrange them. I tell myself that it's the hall table or the dining-room shelves that need a change, but the truth is, I'm the one that does. It could be a late-winter craving for the onset of spring, or a new treasure or a holiday party, that gets me going. I don't think twice about blending new and old, ornate and simple, tall and short. And I never mind about breaking up collections—using silver with tole, mixing porcelain with plants, tucking pictures in among a grouping of figurines. A new shelf or tabletop arrangement always enhances the style of a room—or ever so mischievously alters it.

Use a pedestal or tiered cake stand
to give a display of small items a lift.

ather than lining up a group of these small silver pots and toast racks on my guestroom dresser, *above,* I distributed them casually among other items, creating so much more for the eye to see. This cherished display of white ironstone and transferware, *opposite,* would have been lost in a white corner cupboard. Placed against rich sage green, however, every piece comes across dramatically.

Layer rather than line up items to enhance a display.

A Gracious Setting

These days, when family dining areas are apt to be part of an extended kitchen, the formal dining room too often sits frozen in time, decorated and used only for holidays or a special party. But, whether I'm expecting guests or not, I want my dining room to look festive and inviting at all hours and in all seasons.

As much as I adore elegant candlesticks and fine china, I'm careful not to set a stiff-looking table. That's why coming up with an original centerpiece or sideboard display, often from items already at hand, is as creative for me as cooking is for some of my friends. Using offhand decorative ingredients, as well-balanced as those in a recipe, is my way of relaxing a formal room — and my guests as well.

I find it helps to set a theme for dressing the table. That way, I have something to guide my selection of everything from the linens to the centerpiece. Bunches of white lilac gathered in white ironstone jugs and creamy viburnum in clay pots created a relaxed, country feeling for this spring lunch.

Successful entertaining depends as much on the ambience— the lighting, the table, and so on—as on the food.

centerpieces

WE'VE ALL COME a long way from the days when creating a centerpiece meant plunking down a bowl of flowers and a pair of candle-sticks. Yes, the table should look pretty, but it should also be interesting and maybe even a little surprising. I get endless pleasure from dreaming up arrangements with items that aren't supposed to go together—a simple piece of fruit, a whimsical birdbath, delicate etched glass. A green-and-white pitcher might suggest some moss or ferns; a glass apple might be blended with real ones. It's amazing how a change of context can suddenly make an item seem more sculptural and give it newfound significance.

Most often, I'll find something tall and distinctive for the center of the table. But small decorations that extend the length of the table are lovely, too, such as a line of gourds or china birds alternating with glowing votive candles. Whatever surprises, delights, and pulls the table together in a fresh way can be called a centerpiece.

A weathered urn, a bowl of lemons, a wire tray
can be just as appealing as fine silver.

The chipped little birdbath, *above*, softened with vines and moss, makes a cozy nest for shining gold balls (why use them only at Christmas?) on candy-striped quilting. *Opposite*, plates ready for the salad course join the composition at the center of this table. A mellow autumn gathering, with a casual sprinkling of acorns, uses wooden boxes to elevate gilded and glass pears.

summer buffet luncheon sent me to the kitchen and garden for inspiration, *opposite*. In contrast to the weathered pots brimming with humble ingredients, the arrangement is dressed up with sweet little figurines and a green footed bowl, which picks up a color in the paisley cloth. *Below*, the glazes on the rustic jugs suggested a whole orchard of ideas, from branches of quinces to leafy majolica plates, to serve as holders for birch-bark candles.

Anyone who has been in my home or shopped at my stores knows that I love to layer items and play with colors and textures. Whether I'm serving a simple breakfast, an elegant lunch, or afternoon tea, I'll layer linens and plates on the table. Here, Gretchen pulled out her majolica, which seemed to suit the lighthearted mood of this intimate table for two, while the different textures help set off the china. The wire trays, for example, serve as firm place mats and lend a nice, informal touch.

Use some of your best things —
china, linens, silver —
at least once a day.

When the table has a limited palette, such as the blues and creams *opposite*, you're more free to mix different textural accents at each place setting — a metal napkin holder, some majolica, and a raffia place mat. With a white tablecloth, *above*, it is possible to introduce touches of color with pretty tinted goblets and a centerpiece of subtle hues.

Don't let the table become too stiff or too formal — guests should feel relaxed.

table linens

IT DOESN'T MATTER whether you have a formal dining room or a table in the kitchen, and it doesn't matter what the meal or the occasion—pretty table linens transform every gathering. They offer the chance to make each dinner party, each family celebration, special and a little bit different from the last.

Some of the linens I've collected are specifically suited to favorite sets of china, and a few cotton prints I cherish are meant for summertime suppers on the porch. But I've also fallen for tablecloths, place mats, and odd sets of napkins for no other reason than that they are luscious or fun or unusual. (From time to time, I've even enlisted a matelassé coverlet or an embroidered curtain panel as table dressing.) And I'm not one bit shy about mixing them up.

Napkins needn't match the table in color if they match in spirit.

napkins
3 ways

I think of napkins as being like scarves—stylish accents that can complete a look. Pleated inside a wine goblet, hat-folded on top of a plate, or belted by a ring, napkins are what diners reach for first. Be imaginative: Open their eyes before they open their napkins.

❋1 FOLDED INTO AN EASEL, a starched white linen napkin becomes an elegant placecard holder, *opposite.* To create the pocket, fold the top and bottom edges halfway toward the center, starch and iron, fold into a narrow rectangle and then in quarters to form the easel.

❋2 SNOWY MONOGRAMMED LINEN, *above,* feels as rich as it looks. Tucked suggestively under the first-course salad plate, this weighty napkin seems to reach out to the diner.

❋3 SOFT AS A SUMMER SCARF, the sunny napkin topping a tray of majolica plates, *right,* is much prettier fanned loosely through a napkin ring than rolled tight.

Nothing is less conducive to good entertaining than a stiff, formal setting, so I like to mix artful and artless elements on my sideboard to prevent the room from appearing too formal. Combining an Italian charger with gourds, *opposite*, makes this autumn display as evocative as the painting. When I replace the painting with a mirror, *above*, I like to create a multilevel display to capture the reflections. Here, with baskets and books as platforms, hurricane candles and tiny spring bouquets step up and down like the notes of a song.

candlelight
3 ways

For me, an evening gathering just wouldn't be complete without the romantic glimmer of candles—especially beautiful against the chocolate-brown walls of our dining room. I can't resist collecting pretty candleholders of all types and using several at once. Even in daytime, handsome ones in glass or silver glow.

※1 THE MULTIPLE REFLECTIONS cast by glass and silver create such an angelic radiance that my feeling is, the more the better. At a winter cocktail party, *opposite,* I added glass candlesticks, hurricanes, and etched-glass bottles to flickering votives and placed them on silver stands for extra gleam.

※2 MY SIDEBOARD, *above,* all but calls out for impressive candlesticks. I'd rather use a candelabra as a crowning flourish here than on the dinner table, where they might block guests' views of one another.

※3 A HOLIDAY TRENCHER, of crimson apples, pine garland, and silver candelabra holding tall, slender tapers, *right,* makes this centerpiece a moveable feast.

The Garden Room

Some of my happiest and most relaxed hours are spent on the porch

overlooking our garden. Sweet air and fresh fragrances surround me, and I feel

utterly comfortable and sheltered, only feet from the catbird caroling in a bush.

From the moment it's warm enough to have breakfast here, through warm summer

evenings and well into autumn, this is the casual center of our home life.

A porch offers the best of two worlds—a place to let the outdoors move in

and interior comforts move out. As it's probably the least formal gathering place in

a house, it's definitely a room for creature comforts: chairs with deep cushions,

simple tables that can take a tray of drinks or a pair of tired feet, pillows for

lounging and napping. Since we often have dinners on our porch on warm evenings,

I use a tall dresser for storing crockery, linens, and vases. I leave the decoration

to nature: flowers and plants, of course, but also longer-lasting branches,

potted herbs, and baskets of seashells and pinecones.

I consider the porch my warm-weather living room, almost like a vacation version of the real thing just inside. The sofa and chairs are simple dark wicker, but they're softened and brightened with a cheerful mix of fabrics and plenty of cushions. The "coffee tables" are just a pair of inexpensive wicker boxes that are easily moved. I use the tall screen to hide watering cans, pots, and garden tools—all out of sight until needed. Every room needs at least one mirror, so I hung three little ones on the screen to reflect the garden light.

Have plenty of storage for extra glasses, linens, and flatware, as well as warm blankets and throws for cool evenings.

indoors/out

THERE'S JUST SOMETHING about a porch that encourages easy sociability and good conversation. Even if I'm throwing a formal party, I have my guests start out on our screened-in porch; they seem to mingle and relax so much better there. I keep plantings low on the outside of the room, or several feet away from it — porches are prone to dampness, and this allows for the best possible air circulation. For the same reason, I like the space to be relatively uncluttered. I chose just a few pieces of wicker and bamboo furniture, which are both practical and light in appearance; this way the airiness of the space — and, for that matter, the garden — can be appreciated. Everything from the slipcovers to the side tables to the floor is washable. And the lighting couldn't be simpler: Once the sun goes down, masses of flickering votives cast a magical spell over the room. That's all the light you need to sit and talk by late into the night.

To enhance candlelight, group several votives in front of — or even on top of — a mirror.

A tiered silver tray, *opposite*, turns a collection of sand dollars and white shells into confections. *Below*, an autumn symphony seemed to assemble itself from like-minded ingredients: A gardener's tray and baskets, as well as a birdhouse on this old pewter cake stand, make a rich, woodsy display.

The shapes and textures of nature make especially fine decorations on the porch.

To read, snooze, or just idle a summer afternoon away on the porch with friends, there's nothing like a cozy, cottony sofa or chaise with all the comfort and good looks you'd want in any room, *above*. Crisp, colorful — and properly treated — pretty slipcovers make porch furniture practical and inviting, *opposite*.

Refuge and Retreat

❧ⱿⱿⱿ❧

I'm convinced that bedrooms have magical healing powers. As an escape

from the day's demands, this room of quiet and comfort is more restorative to me

than any mythical fountain of youth. When I slip under the quilt and

sink into the pillows with a book, tensions dissolve. At the first light of morning,

I awake somehow filled with new energy, fresh ideas.

However much we take care of others all day, the bedroom is one place

to which we can retreat and take care of ourselves. For me, that means surrounding

myself with little luxuries—flowers, a soft throw, a silky pillow, a scented candle,

elegant sheets. Even color, whether chosen to cheer or to soothe, is a far

more personal matter here than in public rooms. Though many things in my

bedroom never change, including treasured photos and mementos, I do enjoy

changing the bed's wardrobe with the seasons.

A small bedroom can have as much style as a large one, especially if the details are kept simple and tailored and the furnishings are multifunctional. Decorating this one for our daughter, Kelly, was a special pleasure for me. To punch up the bed's strong black scrolls, I used lots of pure white linen with black accents. Some mirrored vanity trays I've collected over the years found an unexpected new home on the wall. Since space is at a premium, Kelly's cubbied desk serves a multitude of purposes, keeping both necessities and personal treasures — such as a box of her great-great grandmother's letters — close at hand.

All bedside furniture needs plenty of drawers or shelves.

bed linens

"HOME TO BED"—I just love the sound of that phrase. There's certainly no piece of furniture more consoling than one's own bed. So it's only natural that the more complicated and harried people's lives become, the more they choose to indulge in luscious bedding, from the sheets through layers of cuddly blankets, duvets, quilts, bed skirts, and shams.

The bed, of course, sets the tone—subdued or colorful, contemporary or romantic—for the rest of the room and its mood can be altered simply through the choice of linens and pillows. I don't want dressing the bed to become a time-consuming chore, but I'm drawn to scads of different pillows, from big Euroshams to little bolsters to make the bed inviting and luxurious. For a less romantic and more streamlined look, I might remove the decorative pillows and make the linens themselves the accent by creating a generous turnback of the sheets and duvet. Whether you like scintillating damask or cotton ticking (or both), what matters is that the fabrics and pillows you choose bring pleasure to you and vitality to the room. After all, it's not only sensuous comfort we crave here but beauty as well.

Fabric textures—soft, tactile, inviting—are more important in the bedroom than anywhere else.

dressing the bed
3 ways

My philosophy of bed-making? More is definitely more. A bed should be lush and make you want to curl up under its covers, a look best achieved in my opinion by layering prints, patterns, and pillows.

❋ **1** **RED AND BLACK** form a merry dance of patterns from ticking to plaid to paisley, *left.* The coverlet's ruffle overlays a contrasting bed skirt, making the bed seem higher.

❋ **2** **FOR SUMMERTIME,** the same bed dresses lightly in a chintz of pale roses, *above.* To punch up the dust ruffle and shams of the same print, a large pillow sham in a Provençal print and black-backed needlepoint pillow were added.

❋ **3** **A VIVID COLOR SCHEME** unites gentle florals and two toiles with bold accent bands of pink, *opposite.* The black-and-white toiles click smartly with the wallpaper, and notes of pink and green in the ruffles and quilting exude a sunny cottage feel.

The playful version of an old-fashioned canopy bed on these pages has such an airy architecture that it really needs nothing to enhance it — except perhaps the painted flourishes on the wall. In winter, *above*, an embroidered bolster and piles of perky pillows provide a touch of drama. Summertime, *opposite*, calls for romance: The palette changes to ethereal whites, and sheer scarf panels casually looped and tied over the canopy turn the bed into a dreamboat adrift among the clouds.

pillows
3 ways

I love the way that pillows can instantly change the look of a bed and like to have plenty on hand just for that purpose. Often it's their dressmaker details—fringe, flange, pleating, buttons and bows—that give them their style and charm.

✻1 STRIPES AND CHECKS are natural partners, but rarely so smartly combined as on this set of pillows, *left*. The bold black piping on the box pillow and the bolster's brush fringe provide a graphic transition between strong, contrasting fabrics.

✻2 A FAMILY OF TOILES, *above*, for a bed, headboard, and pillows is accented with compatible trims. Emphasizing the femininity of this look, the middle pillow sports a buttoned, ruffled-edge belt that repeats the tiny checks in the border.

✻3 A LOW-KEY MEDLEY of unmatched shams and pillows, *opposite*, came together bit by bit. All was soft pastels and silky finishes until a pair of rabbits added a lively touch of whimsy.

windows

LIKE MOST PEOPLE, the moment I walk into a room my eye is naturally drawn to the windows. How they're dressed affects not only the light but also the decorative feeling of the room. I tend to prefer uncomplicated window treatments, the kind that aren't so theatrical or fussy that they draw attention away from more significant elements, such as art or furnishings. I do like softness and privacy in the evening, with perhaps a touch of luxury, but by day I want full sunlight.

Before making a choice, consider the size of the windows, what direction they face, what the view is, and if neighbors are part of the picture. Your answers will determine whether you need window dressings for privacy, for light control, or simply to complete the look of the room. Sometimes it turns out that the right solution is no curtains at all; perhaps just a shade or shutters will do.

Be generous with curtain fabric. Gathered at the sides or puddled on the floor, extra material imparts a luxurious feel at little cost.

curtains

3 ways

Dressing the windows to complement your room is like choosing the right shoes or purse to go with an outfit. Whether you choose a dressy or simple style, custom or ready-made, curtains provide a perfect opportunity to be inventive. Even subtle variations in fabrics and details can add to the look.

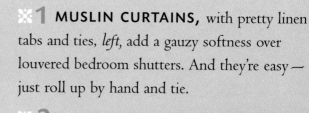

1 MUSLIN CURTAINS, with pretty linen tabs and ties, *left,* add a gauzy softness over louvered bedroom shutters. And they're easy — just roll up by hand and tie.

2 READY-MADE BURLAP PANELS — yes, burlap! — *above,* have been delicately smocked to gather the tops, blending innocence with earthiness. Natural-looking burlap has a lovely drape and is sheer.

3 SOFT UPHOLSTERY FABRICS, such as this sage-green damask, hang beautifully and need no lining. My friend Judy simply draped and knotted two lengths over a curtain rod to instantly create an elegant treatment, *opposite.*

bedside table
3 ways

Any surface handy to the bed can serve as a bedside table. And who says you need two identical ones? I like appealing objects as well as merely useful ones to add their graceful note at bedside and, always, some fresh flowers or greenery.

※1 A LADY'S DESK, *opposite,* is my absolute favorite solution for bedside furniture. It fills so many purposes at once: organized catchall, treasure chest, and writing center.

※2 THIS TROLLEY CART on castors, *above,* is easy to move aside. Two lower shelves free the top for a romantic arrangement, complete with a candle and sweet-scented lily of the valley.

※3 DELIGHT GUESTS, *right,* by displaying a pretty collection next to their bed. These elegant enamel boxes are captured on an amber glass tray and under a bell jar.

aking a guest room truly inviting is an ideal opportunity to indulge one's own fancies. Here, pampering, comfort, and warmth are all that matter; beyond plenty of good towels and some small bottles of toiletries, practicalities need not intrude. My own guest room, *right,* with its slipcovered love seat, tea things, and piles of good books, allows guests to while away some private time in complete comfort.

Spend a night
    in your own guest room.

Nell Hill's Decorating Secrets

When it comes to decorating, I don't believe in

hard-and-fast rules—it's just too personal for that.

In the end, I think surrounding yourself with what you love

and what makes you happy is right. But over the years I've

learned so much from Nell Hill's shoppers and friends

whose homes I admire, and I've discovered some useful

insights and ideas. I'm fortunate also to have my own

"design laboratory" at my stores, somewhere I can

experiment and try things out almost on a daily basis.

On the following pages I've gathered together many

of the decorating observations, hints, and suggestions

I've picked up along the way. I've often found

them helpful. I hope you will, too.

Unlocking the Secrets

Starting out

SEVEN BASICS
TO KEEP IN MIND

✳ **FOCUS ON ONE THING**

Build a room around a focal point,
whether it's the fireplace, a beautiful sofa,
or a generous kitchen table.

✳ **BE PRACTICAL**

Rooms are to be lived in. If furniture
blocks traffic or doorways, if the arrangement of chairs isn't sociable, if there's not
enough storage—it doesn't matter if the
room looks good, the design isn't right.

✳ **KEEP IT SIMPLE**

I like to have lots of things around me to
engage the eye, but if a room has too
much going on or requires too much effort
to keep up, it's not working. Pare down by
removing all the inessentials, then build up
gradually until a balance is achieved.

✳ **CONSIDER THE SCALE**

Play with scale in a room. Don't be afraid
to use large pieces in small rooms. A single
large armoire or a tall palm will give a
modest space height and importance.

No solution works for everyone.

✦ Relax a formal room,
dress up a plain one. ✦

✳ PLAN LONG-TERM

When it comes to the big decisions—
furniture such as a sofa and large
armchairs, or bed—ask yourself: Will I
like this as well in July as I do in
January? Will I still care for it two
years from now?

✳ KEEP EVERYTHING FLEXIBLE

Don't be afraid to change things. No
arrangement should be static—our
rooms should be as fluid and flexible
as our lives. In small spaces, try to use
furniture that plays more than one
role—a chest that serves both as storage
and a table, for example.

✳ MIX IT UP

Pairs of matching chairs are fine, but
matching sets of furniture need variety.
Once the larger pieces are set,
introduce a few quirky items—an ornate
console behind a sofa or a side table made
from a garden urn, for instance.

Introducing color

EIGHT TIPS ON PAINT AND FABRIC

❋ MAINTAIN A BALANCE

Lots of pattern or color in a room can overwhelm. If there's already plenty of pattern, perhaps in an oriental rug or curtains, use a neutral color for the sofa and other large furnishings.

❋ THINK WHITE

I love white but a little variety will make it much more interesting. Even "white" rooms can have contrasting variations on walls, ceiling, and trim. Try using different shades, from ivory to pearl to linen, and different finishes—semigloss next to matte.

❋ CONSIDER NEUTRALS

Colors with subtle undertones—beige, sage green, dove gray, putty—are generally more restful on the walls than purer hues. Moreover, they won't compete with any accent colors you may introduce in accessories.

❋ THINK TEXTURE

Fabrics that people love to touch—with nap, nubble, or sheen—are especially important in neutrals, because they vary the way light is reflected.

❋ THINK SCALE

Large rooms, like large pieces of furniture, can usually take more color and pattern than smaller ones. Fewer colors will make small rooms feel larger.

Colors are often more interesting when they harmonize rather than match perfectly.

Limiting your color palette allows you to introduce more pattern in a room.

✳ THINK PATTERN

Fabric patterns should suit the scale of the piece. A big, bold print, for example, will probably overwhelm a small armchair.

✳ THE RIGHT STRIPE

Striped and checked fabrics are wonderful almost anywhere. Pinstripe, ticking, or gingham can be casual or formal, and are all good choices to tame busy florals.

✳ TRY OUT SWATCHES

Always look at color or fabric samples in the room in which you plan to use them. Bring home good-sized swatches or paint a sample board or area on a wall and study how it appears in different light and at different times of day.

Letting in the light

FOUR LESSONS ON LAMPS

✳ **DON'T OVERDO IT**

Often, less light is better than more. Too much can feel harsh and cold. I generally prefer to have several localized pools of light in a room in place of an overhead source — they make the room both more inviting and more intimate.

✳ **BE TASK-SPECIFIC**

Consider what the purpose of the lamp is and adjust the light accordingly. For working or reading, you want strong and even illumination, but for some situations the atmospheric glow of a low-watt bulb — 40W or even 25W — is preferable.

✳ **USE LAMPS AS ACCENTS**

Use lighting as an accent throughout the house. Shapely floor and table lamps are among my favorite accessories. Use them to lend height, light, and color to a tabletop or sideboard or to bring a forgotten corner to life.

✳ **TWO'S COMPANY**

Pairs provide a fine formal touch to a console table, sideboard, or mantel. (You can make two similar-looking lamps into a pair by giving them matching shades.) Equally decorative — almost like art — are paired wall sconces, an ideal choice for bracketing a mirror or for lighting hallways and other areas where table space is limited.

FIVE LOOKS
FOR WINDOWS

❋ BREAK THE RULES

Use luxurious fabrics in an unexpectedly
casual way. A curtain can be as simple as
an unpleated panel hung from a ring rod;
if the fabric has weight and drape, you
needn't even line it. Or forget rings and
clips altogether and simply loop and knot
a single panel, scarf style, over a half-rod
for a one-sided drop.

❋ INCLUDE DRESSMAKER DETAILS

Try adding a pleated flange in a tiny,
contrasting stripe or attaching the curtain
top with buttoned tabs or bow ties instead
of rings; consider adding a solid ribbon
border to tie in room colors, or putting on
a trim of fringe, or using a different print
for the lining.

❋ MAKE SHEER SENSE

Combine sheers for atmosphere with
shades for privacy so you have the option
of admitting as much light as possible.
Some sheers have subtle patterns or
embroidery, and they come in many
diaphanous colors other than whites.

❋ GO THE LENGTH

Floor-length curtains are generally con-
sidered more formal, suitable for a living
room or dining room. But there are no
fixed rules; generally, I prefer longer
curtains because they visually enlarge
your impression of the windows.

❋ RAISE YOUR SIGHTS

Hang the curtain rod a few inches above
the window frame to visually enlarge the
window and raise the height of the ceiling.

*Use lighting as a decorative accent
as well as a functional element.*

Showing off

SIX IDEAS FOR COLLECTIONS

✳ **COLLECT WHAT YOU LOVE**

Whether it's cookie jars or antique doorstops, it is the passion of the collector that brings a collection to life. Don't be afraid to buy something quirky. Old paintings and vintage photographs can be had for bargain prices at flea markets and yard sales. Choose a topic—pet portraits, flowers, or old houses—and build your own gallery.

✳ **CHECK YOUR CUPBOARDS**

Undiscovered collections are probably sitting in your cupboards and closets. They needn't have great value to have impact—simple items, such as vintage egg cups, birch-bark souvenirs, or even seashells gathered on various vacations can be captivating in a group.

✳ **MATCH AND MIX**

A collection doesn't have to be composed of similar objects; sometimes just one common feature can make all the pieces work—various urn-shaped objects, for example, ranging from an alabaster lamp to a silver trophy to glassware or pieces of the same color, such as celadon pottery.

✳ **PRETTY BEATS PERFECT**

If you have something beautiful, it doesn't matter if it has a chip or a little wear.

✳ **CHOOSE YOUR SPOT**

Where and how a collection is displayed can make all the difference. Glass and silver are best positioned near a window or a table lamp, where they can catch the light. A trio of transferware plates may be lost in a large room yet be a stunning grouping hung together in a small powder room.

✳ **EDIT FOR EFFECT**

Be selective. The best collections are usually not about quantity.

Six Display Secrets

✳ KEEP A FOCUS

Build a display around one or two main items, then add things one at a time. When in doubt, simplify.

✳ REDEFINE LOCATION

Look for less obvious places than tables or bookshelves for displays: Maybe there's a plain-looking corner that needs something bold or gleaming to draw the eye. The tops of kitchen cupboards and armoires can be great places to prop graphic decorative items.

✳ CONSIDER THE BACKGROUND

Anything placed in front of a mirror will have a doubled effect, so keep those compositions simple. Choose items with beautiful profiles to place in front of a window, where they will be silhouetted dramatically. Dark backgrounds, of course, will show off light-colored items and vice versa.

✳ BE FLEXIBLE

If the space you choose for a display is sometimes needed for other purposes, such as a dining table, put your grouping on a tray that can be whisked away at a moment's notice.

✳ THINK SINGLE

Using a strong central shape or grouping on or above the mantel draws and raises the eye, and gives you freedom to play around it imaginatively. Besides the conventional painting or beautifully framed mirror, consider other objects, from architectural fragments to an arrangement of tall grasses to an old toy sailboat.

✳ DRAW FROM DAILY LIFE

Try mixing your finery with the everyday—your best crystal with a scattering of pinecones, or a piece of art with a bowl of apples—to keep the mantel from becoming too formal. Just make sure the elements are related in some way—a repetition of color, shape, or texture will make for a more pleasing composition.

*Oversized mats add weight
and drama to small pictures.*

FIVE ART LESSONS

✳ MAKE A STATEMENT

Group pictures over a sofa or use them
to frame a bed, to give them and the
furniture more presence. Bracketing a
small window or door can actually make it
seem larger. If the room needs a vertical
accent, stack the pictures high to draw the
eye upward. For impact, keep groupings
fairly tight.

✳ BREAK THE MOLD

Unless the focus is a set of matched
prints, avoid combining frames or objects
of the same scale; it can look monotonous.
Balance a vertical with a horizontal; blend
a big rectangular picture with a small
square tray or an oval mirror. Don't worry
about mixing gilded or silvery frames in a
room or using an unframed canvas here
and there.

✳ FIND NEW PLACES

Try a mirror on the staircase to amplify
the light, or perhaps a bold picture to
provide a focal point at the top of the
landing. To give a narrow wall importance,
fill it with an oversized framed piece. If
you have high ceilings, dress the space
above a door frame — a great spot for a
row of pretty plates.

✳ TRY IT OUT

To avoid misplaced nail holes, draw the
grouping of art to scale on graph paper
first; or cut brown-paper shapes of the
pictures and tape them on the wall before
sinking a single nail.

✳ CREATE OPPORTUNITIES

I like to use vertical plate racks, carved
bracket shelves, or molding strips around
the house. They provide a wonderful stage
for arrangements that can be changed
seasonally or at a moment's notice.

Dressing up

THREE LOOKS
FOR THE BED

✳ CREATE LAYERS

Don't hide fine monogrammed or hem-
stitched sheets under a coverlet. For a
pretty, three-part surface, fold the coverlet
back a full third to expose the top of the
sheets, then place a rolled or folded quilt
at the foot of the bed.

✳ MIX IT UP

Bed pillows and shams are like the toppings
on a sundae—rich and indulgent. To get
this effect, use a mix of textiles and textures—anything from satin with cotton to
damask with toile—to enliven the bed. To
harmonize a double bed (or larger), pair
the bigger shams and repeat some pillow
prints elsewhere, in the trim on a duvet or
another pillow, perhaps, or the bed skirt.

✳ TRY ON A DUVET

Duvet covers aren't just for comforters.
They offer a quick way to protect your
old quilt or blanket or to change its
look—and the look of your room—
entirely. How about a sexy silk duvet, or
a bright plaid with big black buttons?

*Dressing the bed in eye-catching,
sumptuous linens will distract from the
scale of a small room.*

NINE IDEAS
FOR THE TABLE

❉ ADD HEIGHT

Use more than one centerpiece to
visually anchor a very long table. As long
as they don't interfere with guests' line
of vision, try cake stands, compotes,
tiered trays, small terracotta pots, or urns
piled with anything from fresh fruit to
Christmas balls.

❉ DRAW FROM NATURE

Consider whatever's in season to decorate
the table—fresh fruit, sprigs of spring
blossoms, tiny pots of fresh herbs, even
fresh artichokes. Instead of confining
them to a bowl, let them spill down the
center of the table. Don't be afraid to mix
in artificial fruits—carved wood, glass,
or ceramic—with the real things.

❉ CREATE HARMONY

Keeping colors harmonious is just as
important on a tabletop as it is in a room
as a whole. I might let favorite crockery, a
tablecloth, or even a certain texture, such
as polished wood or glass, inspire the
color palette.

❉ GET PERSONAL

Put a "centerpiece" at each place setting.
They needn't even be the same; alternate
tiny bouquets or potted herbs, china
birds, or votives set in a ribbon-tied spray
of foliage.

❉ BEGIN WITH NEUTRALS

Basics should be as much a part of your
table's wardrobe as they are of yours.
That includes linens, whites as well as
solid colors that complement the china
you most often use. This gives you greater
freedom to accessorize.

❋ NOW EXPAND YOUR OPTIONS

Use tablecloths by any other name to introduce a fresh look: a white Provençal quilt, an embroidered coverlet, a toile curtain panel, even a plaid blanket. To my mind, almost any appealing textile is fair game for a table covering.

❋ ADD DRESSY DETAILS

To alleviate the prim look of fine tablecloths, try layering the linen with a drifty organza overskirt or a colored cloth laid on the diagonal—lovely on a round table. For festive events, tie the corner drops of a rectangular cloth with ribbon bows. You might even tuck in a spray of flowers. Or add a lustrous brocade runner down the center of the table.

❋ DON'T MAKE DO, MAKE IT

If shopping doesn't yield the style or color of tablecloth you want, search out the riches of a fabric store, then have your choice cut and hemmed to the right size. (Always carry the dimensions of your dining table with you; you never know when something irresistible will turn up.) If a cloth you love is too small for your table, add a new border all around.

❋ USE NAPKINS AS ACCENTS

Mixing sets of napkins, or alternating two strong solid colors, can add spark to an informal table. Crisp linen hand towels, embroidered vintage ones, or beautifully detailed fingertip towels also make delightful serviettes.

Index

Acknowledgments

This book showcases the work of many people, but I would like to single out several to whom I am particularly grateful: Kim Waller, who co-wrote this book; Charles Riley, who helped style the photographs; and Bryan McCay, whose superior photography continues to amaze me in our third collaboration. Their talent and enthusiasm made this project exciting and personally fulfilling. Many thanks to John Smallwood, who assembled this team; I continue to be proud to be included among his company's titles. I also want to thank Jill Cohen, Karen Murgolo, Kristen Schilo, and everyone at my publisher, Bulfinch Press, for supporting this project from the beginning. Finally, my deepest gratitude to Jean Lowe for her sage advice, boundless energy, and belief in me every step of the way.

My three stores are built on my wonderful employees: Emily Armstrong, Kathleen Armstrong, Glenna Batchelder, Jenny Bell, Sue Bell, George Bilimek, Stephanie Bottinger, Heather Brown, Carolyn Campbell, Ethel Campbell, Suzy Clayton, Shirley Cline, Joyce Colman, Abigail Compton, Chubby Darrenkamp, Joe Domann, Barbara Fricke, Judy Green, Carol Hale, Gail Hanson, Paige Haynes, Nikki Heiman, Vicky Hinde, Jo Hines, Christian Holmes, Debbie Hooper, Zachary Hoyt, Dillon Kinsman, Joy Kromer, Pat Kuckleman, Amber Kuhnert, Ruth Kunkle, Nichole Liggett, Penny Linscott, Doe Loftus, June Lynn, Mike Maples, Chance Massey, Jackie McClellan, Shannon Mize, Gloria Nash, Lori Newton, Lois Nieman, Sara Nolting, Cheryl Owens, Heather Owens, Justin Reuter, Jamie Servaes, John Shackleford, Kathy Sledd, Elizabeth Smith, Angela Steubs, Matt Stout, Gretchen Sullivan, Kerri Wagner, Geri Weishaar, Marceline Weishaar, Jan Wessel, Lindsey Wietharn, Bill Wilson, Cyreesa Windsor, Kay Wolfe.

Numerous friends were also generous with their time: Kim Amick, Marsee Bates, Merrilee Bozzoli, Carol Burns, Joan Carpenter, Gloria Case, Averie Chapman, Barbara Cosgrove, Lynda Coulter, Melinda DiCarlo, Deann Dunn, Kelly Ediger, Robyn Enright, Brenda Graves, Cheryl Hartell, Carol Housh, Ann Humphreys, Morgan Knipp, Melanie Krumbholz, Evelyn Monea, Nancy Neary, Charlene Roberts, Greg and Nan Sigman, Neil and Gretchen Sullivan, Laurie Wilson, Tom and Sylvia Zinn.

M.C.G.